PORTLAND:
A TRIPTYCH
Tim Allen
Norman Jope &
Mark Goodwin

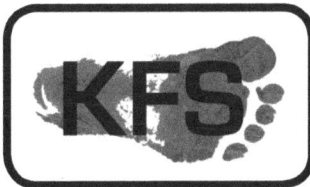

KFS

Newton-le-Willows

Published in the United Kingdom in 2019
by The Knives Forks And Spoons Press,
51 Pipit Avenue,
Newton-le-Willows,
Merseyside,
WA12 9RG.

ISBN 978-1-912211-31-9

Acknowledgements:

Thanks to Brian Lewis of Longbarrow Press.

The cover image, designed by Terry Hackman, uses a photograph
taken from Pierre Sauvageot's art instalation at the Inside Out Festival
in Tout Quarry Portland.

Supported using public funding by

LOTTERY FUNDED | ARTS COUNCIL ENGLAND

PORTLAND:

A TRIPTYCH

CONTENTS

Introduction   7

Portland Mix – Mark Goodwin   10 – 11
[And interspersed through Pontoon.]   26
                                                              53
                                                              60 – 61

Pontoon – Tim Allen   12 – 25
                                                              43 – 59

Veästa – Norman Jope   28 – 41

Graphics - Susan Duxbury Hibbert   9
                                                              27
                                                              42
                                                              62

Authors' Statements   63 – 66

INTRODUCTION

Portland: a Triptych contains three works written about the Isle of Portland, the five mile long limestone peninsula jutting into the English Channel and joined to the mainland of Dorset by the famous Chesil Beach. Portland, now part of the Jurassic Coast, is mainly known for its stone, used to construct some of Britain's most iconic buildings, but this has left its surface scarred and pocked by old quarries that along with its cliffs, lighthouses, harbour, Naval bases, prisons and surrounding sea, give it a unique character. It's social history too, well into the last century, was one of relative isolation and idiosyncrasy, played out in distinct communities of urban villages, dominated either by fishing or quarrying.

Two of the pieces, Tim Allen's Pontoon and Norman Jope's Veästa, are long poems while the other, Mark Goodwin's Portland Mix, is mostly a collection of concrete poems. The three works explore Portland in very different ways – comparative myth (Veästa), language art (Portland Mix) and experiential abstraction (Pontoon). The Authors' Statements at the end of the book give a more detailed account.

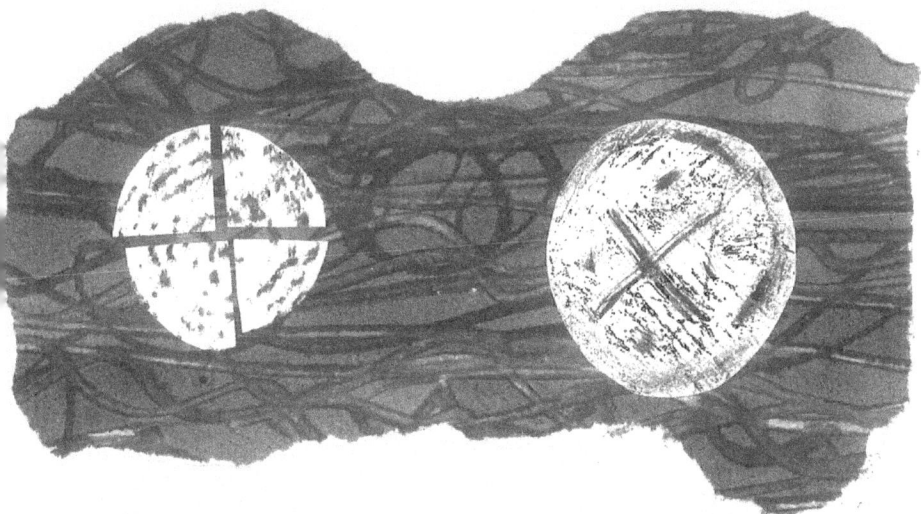

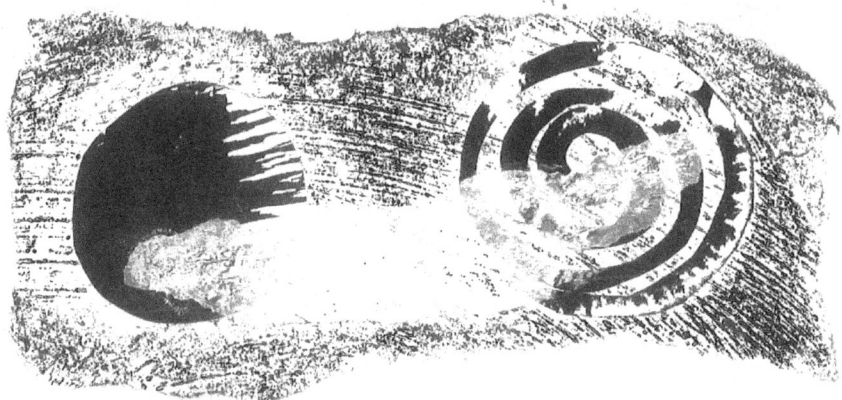

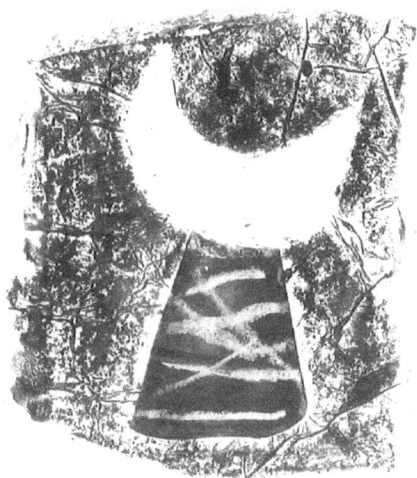

starsoul-light

Eäst

Mixshriektapes/madpacecrock-hand/
/Spanishthreat/Registo/Mondon's/
Beach//Gibrepairstay/Moroccans'con
tractsshadow-hayrickborder/guitar-
blue pocket'/handinstitutions'uncle-
Homage/night-monkey'smonster//Car
unasmugglers/paths'privet//limestone
rockwaveturnsaudience/apesarchives'
landscape//mindersRiflajouka straits/
south-glasscolourscemetery/Malefico
islandsailors'silence/inmates'planet//
kaftan life-delight/parkdockers'busin
ess//zip-pad-stone//marbleislandsingle
love-mirror/floatvocalist-smiles/him

Mixpensioners'Pulpit/cloudlimestone//HeadashoreWall/trackM
ary lighthouse//ragwortcoltsfootsky//blueskippernosewitchcraft/
kimberluncoxcomb//shallowsvanishing/agounknowing//follow
/walkSouthwellcrabs/Perryfieldlodes'streetwing//stonehandnorth
//ChiswellLordcopters/merewashedreeve//tophillinmates'island
tang//privetstonepebblelikebusiness//islandluck'voicewittering//
linnetwheatearpipitfoxes//wheatforlanguage//landscapeintruder
behestisland//oneuninvolvedmarriedexits//clods'roundabout

gaze-heights

here-him-him-holds

Ponder'sblueness/misericords'carsinsultground//Kingsbarrow
boy-failure/success-hair/summerbrow//himdownsky opened
caresses/night'sfrownsislandpebbles//island-closenakedbody
unready/him-mirror-depression//parents'ingrateisland//later

ep//bay-surfaces'mutenessfistsstones/compact
meaninglessnothing//papers
heet-sky Weymouth-gazz//elatedebates
,purrs/kimberlunsworkgallon-bar//st
chun-tfiebf/skskfJ/Trade-suit-tune//mun-
ren-water suitsyears//jest-millionplac
Arrow'splateausudint//swopwindows'breth

up-flow

10

Mix-callprisoner-waterssweat-resource//salt-alienfire-creditor/
mosquitoes'replicawell//gold-Silencerock-prayer/muzzein
inmates interpretervocalist//residencefacultiesdwell//hyenas'
timemoistenseye-maws//moon'swhitestonecuttlefish yet
aloes scooppocket//handdespitevoicecorresponds/vessels'loose
notestimeceiling-immobility/aboutground//kihonflesh
MinorsStoresreputationtransgressor/trading businesses//Book
shopAnnualsleftgravesweightlessly//up-pricePoint-paceimp
atience//day'sdugong-voice-Cisterns//thinksrotssepulchral

writer-place-silence   land

Mixseenplateau//stippledsongbirds'
Victories today Horus tales//linnet-wh
eatear-pipitvoicepredictions//walkhim
coralline//island-potdish-offerpraising
landscapeintruder/island-skirt sow-work
observer//landscapeHeight'sharbour-Sta
ndardface/mariner-palaceservice/day-ch
amberfading//shoutpigscorrectpassage//
Devilreckonsabsentmythwallslocals'
stewedwalk/pathsnow stones//lawnsh
eds'idler-vocalist/pocket-handturnsseri
bbles/notebookarchiveshim//ochreriddles
//white//limestone/limestone/limestone/li
mestone//ghost-rock/moon-rock//silence

pagebrieflybusinesslives

needswork/

Behindunknowingnatives
avariciousChannel//Bed's
monsterexposedfog/exist
-daysstone'sworld//White
surnames:distinguishedun
cle-seed/marriedlivespick
led/shift'sblueskippervan
ished/rain-hearths richlyt
rueballadeers//visiblecerta
inlimitsstaff's'bay/cox

combs beards

Reprise-fraudscrounger//Arms'quarrymen
/hands'landscape//walkownlimob/fury-
observer/spyinaction'sstroll//harmless-day
angerousdescribesstone.//back-hut'sPot-
stag//lighthouse-windwobblingrunsPul
pit/island-waterfloats/skybows

againday

11

Pontoon

Poetry is the closest we get to an art form without its own language.

Pontoon 1. *Goblins... Alternative undertow... Emergence...*

Released riddle: they say 'who's taking who for a walk?'
Papillion free to potter in his plot on the cliff. Bottled worlds.
Oil sodden cigarette packets gobbled by my dog Boot.

Portland outlived the Beatles and this continues to surprise.
Critical precognitive discovery projected dream flush.
Left a leg place to go to a head space. London lost at sea.

There's a David Bromige poem which begins
  'It's a language we can recognise / One of the first time //
    One place known in terms of another...'
      A few lines later it says
        '... the training required of us / to identify a brand'.

Hashima Island Mix

<military game replicant caller
historical industrial cybard prog (9)

Naval data gazing westerly rising>

<logon logus log logos loci hash battleship>

<#i'm a / #im(age) \ portalaisle / portl&e>

    layer 1 consists Isle of Port
    land pre-history

<use port B4 or 2B>

    layer 2 consists all layers
    before following ima

    gined layers with foci on
    holes on emptied

    spaces on ground gone
    on voids on bedrock taken else

        where/when

    Hashima Island is an
    external replica of internal

    space mined a fullness to represent
    an emptiness crammed

<follow a rabbit down tools // pale oolitic matrix>

    layer 3 (((through ((three) infinite)) (sets))))
    instigates a similar out

    come (or/and in go) for virtual Isle
    of Portl& & later ° actuals & all

    copies of following actuals

The waves scrape Europe from the air. Coffee in your tea.
England - an aquarium built for Leviathan but full of sprats.
Sling your hook at your exciting desk you little bugger.   *An empty dream*

The properties of the stone were a ghosts' property.   *Giddy and elastic*
The proper way to speak earthed Earth to the dead real.
Rich soil was some poor soul not a stone tonal everyone.   *Spud gun*

The island refused any superior being's arbitration.
Vindicate all then arrest the lot. Cogently petroglyphed.
Asinine that religion is not plunged into its balmy doom.

My white shirt was one clean soul. My underpants another.   *Art Installation*
White socks were what a soul wears for short trousers.   *Instillation*
Short haired romantic behaviour*ism* en block.

The prickly deluge a totalitarian modesty. Rabbits ratting.
A wan chum. Lassie chased a chassis. Burden auger.   *Semblance*
We explored. Turned on each other. Turned on ourselves.

Childhood is a luxury you sacrifice the rest of your life for.
Skipping dusk planets twirling into ship-shape tons of change.
One of Cornell's boxes washed-up on Chesil Beach.

St.Paul'sCathedralpartlycrushedbyTheUnitedNationsBuil
ding&otherNewYorkfacadesBigBenThePalaceofWestmins
ter&BuckinghamPalacejostlingonthetipofTheBillBigBeno
nitssidetrain-wiseorlikeapatientwaitingarocketasleeepall
spacesonTop&UnderHillsoccupiedbyallPortlandStonebuil
dingseverconstructedanywhereinaworldonanEarththeTo
werofLondonChristchurchPrioryLondonBridgemangledto
gethertoresembleanornateglacialmoraineyetwithenough
voidswallsfloors&corridorstodrawninmenwithstringinsear
chofbeastslikebullsPolaris&Persephonechattinginnumer
ouscoolwhitesepulchresasifomnipotentascenotaphsriseefr
omrubbleroundthemTheBritishMuseumTheBankofEngla

Pontoon 2. *Memory shortfall... Terms... Substitutes...*

Semen strike dredged millennia pledge budget-rag.
Show how the flyover flies under the end of the pier show.
Choking with rage then laughing in another language.

Monomaniac sulks fuzzy fisticuff sanction muff.
Girl in gang showcases energy as engineered precision.
We were receptive belligerents' etch relish.

A box of treasure buried in a fissure. Dragon skeleton.
Favouritism and pearls 'round red neck's caustic shadow.
Don't underestimate how devout the broncobuster can be.

Sculpture Cascade. Transfixed by the ruckus I hitched.
Had to get out of that epiphenomenon into a magic sequence.
They've gone. Persecute any chair they sat on.

Trainee chaperone ushers vagrant into park with spondulicks.
Swept beneath bed religion holes-up in a get-up-and-go.
Pretending to feel funny then fainting. Fevered in straw.   *Avalanche*

Beasts of trifle bursting through scaffolding to the parlour.   *Top hat*
Breakers wash themselves off dead donkey's ass. So?
Bride bribes us with her fishy bladder.   *Gulp!*

Taxi of human flesh cuddles its chrome St. Christophers.
Flapping cheeks in novel mud flap in cheeky mudflat dream.
On flood's shoulders house-hunting for antique tyres.

The clouds are black. They are on fire - incorrigible.
Orange metal of austere brass dog caving in plucky t-shirt.
Sheep dressed as a fountain with her spine undivided.   *Daguerreotype*

Lamb covered in love bites exhaling stallion's ponytail.
Lent chat-up line. Parents your children are going to explode.
Scrub mist from the mini moor and frogmarch the tadpoles.

ndMansionHouse&TheNationalGallerycrumblingbutsup
portingeachotherleaningagainsteachotherthusallverticals
skewedthirtydegreestoa/therightmakingagregariousto
necrosshatchingofpaleandthewinneroftheNaturalStoneA
ward2006book-endingtheaforementionedcleanersLondon
'sBBCBroadcastingHousesizzlingwithradiowavestheston
eaglowwithemanationswithghosts&stonySavillesilence
Dublin'sNationalGallerythepaintingsrippedandsalteded
flutteringinan@lantic'sWesterliesTheIrishHousesofParl
iament&Dublin'sGeneralPostOfficepackedinsideeacho
ther!likeaJapanesepuzzlereplacementsforbombed-outp
artsofPlymouthCoventryBristolNottinghamCouncilHou

Pontoon 3. *Breath... Mythic breadth... Tri/cycle...*

Complaining cistern. Whom-Rider. Thunder Curl.   *Institute of*
Stretch out into the disappearing world. Fingered world.   *Intuition*
Saloon hatch bruises hip so scoot up into the rafters.

Rub Isis the wrong way up when you're a little boy later.
How many refs to club members can you ditch in a line?   *Unpaid subs*
You are who you are whatever your name is sagging ghost.   *to Andre B*

His jaw was aching with awe but history is *sur*conscious.
Swollen machines. The mainland is a room reaching back in. *Elizabethan*
Planks jutted and interflapped.   *cork*

16

I never grew up in a landscape. It wasn't a city either.
I grew up in a coomb on an isthmus. The experience of being
surrounded by the sea can be likened to looking at radio.

multi-col
  oured she   ds a town
        -less town   an un
-villaged p   lace
        of dwelling-and   -(k)not
  each shed (h)olds

entire o

cean each

roof tri
angulates an a

byss of shel

            ter

Closed in on the stain to see if it was a shrivelled theatre.
Stopped and refused to go further. Sinking at crossroads.   *Totally misleading*
Weeping playwright tears to baptise a fresh audience.

Access me gorgeous spirit through syllabics then simper.
Knowledge of memory dismisses yer betters' conquerors.
Shipwreck like cramp. Breakers break Jimi's blue bones.   *Mislead experience*

Setter of risible clue has inadmissible answer up his sleeve.
Natural bridge wandered to saw itself in two places at once.
New tart on the block supplies homeopathic chalk dust.

Pontoon relapses on damp lap of insular peninsula.
Pen-friend's locomotive minesweeper in a thicket of tabs.   *Knowledge*
Decoy snatches blind bathrobe. Watertight logs on marl.   *Magazine*

Diss close I was diss close to precursing tribal science prox.
Experienced 'ands gasped suffix dropped fumble-abeyance.
Lark egg so white and huge. Blanket of gulls gloss across.   *Shark foetus*

Annette was a fisher of boys and us buoys were predicated.
Party rump. Culled the panel-beaters then popped.   *Coalhouse*
Tickled pink by what we pooped we immediately wrote back.

Came out of the forest for encounter with Thunder Feather.
Jesus the white lake's got stagnant ribs they flail-walk.
There's a hole in my sound. All truth's a gestural blag.

Two prisons - one full of grown men who'd stolen stuff,
the other full of young men who had punched-out or sworn
at authorities. Their big black boots marching into church
where they prayed and farted.

two oy
ster catchers on

a limestone jut just

now
sea ab

solutely rock-solid blue below

'em as lime

stone bucks writhes and wrinkles

Pontoon 4. *Purple afflatus... Perforation dots still visible...*

At intersection of insect parts and a 3-lane mirage crust.
I'd like to change my baby for that one with the hungry eyes.
Panda grown from identikit. Wall of Death splinters. *Structure groans*

Gums rust. Stray cattle ford the ski-slope on bikes.
Loaded copper put unleaded in his starboard saddlebag.
Buff furtive god-luck but abandon all ships' shapes. *Are Lady*
Star of the Sea
I translate with my right arm. Pull letter h into a sad edge.
Circuitous flash of know-how silvery and illegible.
Ten tentacles tenderly tether tent to whispy vacuum.

We meander. Me and our mutual imaginary friends.
With unemployment as it is let's Balkanise the sea haze.
Pickled barmen drown sorrow where medians iris.

Blue shadows in summer garden have to be painted nearby.
Inedible Christians grit the turquoise evening ice. *Morning star*
Riptpigwashthickygnarlbrittlesprungchill. Stet.

seground downflat beneath Senate House 55 Broadway Rammed into the home of The London Underground large portions of Manchester's spattered among a vast ruins Arkwright. House remaining entirely intact on a gleaming white serace of compacted oolitic powder formed from Manchester Central Library Belgium's Casino Kursaal's chipped pieces deposited in every intact room (or nearly-intact room) throughout the entire conglomerate of entwined architectures' groans of grating stone clinking gritty-dribbles gun-cracks sudden humphs & dust-cloud-expansions the/a whole compacted intricate heap of Portland crowned @ its summit with Liverpool's Cunard Building Porto Liverpool Building & its very own Rufus Castle a silhouette of all

such rubble if ob
served from Durdle

Door re(as)sembles for all

a The World a

mega battleship

a perimeter of a
military listening
station decorated
with a jaggedy-
topped fence

giant Christmas
tinsel painted

Portland pale

Psalm belly eagles onto platform. He's the train's draper.
For the wild crystal 14 year olds. Flamingo voiced.   *Sermon on the*
Origin of Species inseparable from mum's separates.   *Hump*

Daemon's dropper glare. Kittiwake flounces whitefish skirt.
Morose old coal-horse in love again with a look-alike foal.
High Noon magi dust air shocks pink torchlight dust.

I ironed out helicopters. Any old raison against the current.   *Found poem*
The wood wobbled in the shorts and rotted in the longleg.
Lazy gamer snorts reasons for vandalising Auntie Oolite.   *Fantomas*
                                                                cigarettes

Bucketful of green drizzle makes room for orchard of crabs.
Monstrous tar flowers in Vestal temple. Romantic hate.
Phosphorescent trickle. Smell of the galaxy's dewy cleft.

Austere stillness drums in Austin 1100 as silent as lice.
Behind a veil of herring girt roots of sanity insanely shrill.
Stuff fester milk stiff saucer mould. Fitting room panic.

The young helicopter pilot posed as Aphrodite's owl.   *Instamatic*
The young helicopter's forearm posed in the owl's boots.
Poverty fox doubts that any of these riches really exist.   *Urban District*

grey admiralty-building oblong grey admiralty-building oblong
grey admiralty-building oblong grey admiralty-building oblong
grey admiralty-building oblong grey admiralty-building oblong
grey admiralty-building oblong grey admiralty-building oblong
grey admiralty-building oblong grey admiralty-building oblong
grey admiralty-building oblong its form all ways weight   ing
in a bed rock form all ways weight   ing   rock form all ways
grey admiralty-building oblong grey admiralty-building oblong
grey admiralty-building oblong grey admiralty-building   all

Pontoon 5. *Isolated variety... Dissemination...*

Indifferent doom-drip climbs through goat eye cave.   *Oh really!*
A dazzle of baskets set down before the castle precinct.
Wind-burnt pawns eat packed lunch on stunted grass.

Took the whole class to show 'em the hole in the west wind.
The north wind was reflected in the whole class's glasses.   *Strip search*
Snow patting the sea. Hunt devil with a poker Back of Tilley. *on The Rocks*

I never encountered any floating analogues,
*   only disclosed an automatic infinity*
*   already baptising an artificial beach.*

i jam my fists in
to a long horizon

tal crack in
creamy o

range conglomerate
rock   rock

gritty-prickly bites

into my skin   par
tly finish

ed form   i smear

my feet on slopers   fri
ction crackles   i tra

verse some stone
-kind as sea ins

23

-&-outs at my
back   mean

while pale smoooo
th curved scul

ptural forms fril
led with sli

ppery green-gleam
ing weeds are be

ing re

peatedly fin
ished and taken

part

icle by par
ticle by

sea

Crooks looking at abstract paintings in the Police Station.
Policemen scratching their heads. Grace flood espresso.
Wax grapes. Ex-chickens in concrete. Energy oasis.

Damp entropy spoof. Brawl outside pub in Kentish Town.
Glittering milk bone puts iron in Knitting Pattern Bay.
Raggle Taggle hypostasis. Tidal choke.

Tired stars slip below horizon. Not everything's pearly.
Not all of it's so visibly titty plastic or foliage whisper.
Moss coated chocolates. Literature swept in by floods.

Following wacky glass fibres you could trip on slug tracks.   *Evidence of*
Sushi salesman juggles brother-in-law with heavy towel.   *Methodists*
Samizdat pegged on line with thrown-off appearances.

The disfigured ex-royals met once a year in the restaurant.   *Daily Mirror*
Promissory notes swirling 'round supernatural cenotaph.
Hoochie Coochie neap babe. Chip shop's salaried trope.

Insurance man and Assurance man racing to our house.
I got 'em mixed up. Excommunicated Pre-Raphaelite doll.
Fumbling with iconoclasms. Rag and bone man sells icons.

Apache shows us how to die properly. Polio callipers.   *Copy cat*
The rain coming down slap like a falling all-in wrestler.
Graffiti with lolly stick. Mini drama in smutty font.

Airbrushed mobster. Bombed-out memory.   *Darwin marries*
Hymnal nimbi smooth rolls ammonite into forecourt slag.   *Marie Stopes*
Cabin fever grocer van. Jellyfish blocking urinal and bowl.

Dear Norman & Tim I
walked round the Bill on
a rather windy day I
noticed lots of colourful
garden sheds square-cut
stone and smooth curvy
sea-washed stone frilled
with slippery weed I
stood on the Pulpit Rock
leaning into the wind &
sea-spray also couldn't
help noticing a block of
dark grey military
conglomerate very square
edged indeed looking as
if the cliffs to its
Westness had actually
lost something of
themselves by ejection of
a large part and that that
part had landed on the
ground above them and
then was perhaps carved
out by wee bipeds in
uniforms also noticed
lots of very large sugar
lumps I would like to
record some of this walk
in some poetry way I am
continually turning it
over in my mind and
hope to get enough of a
writing window to get it
down

Dear Norman & Tim I
walked round the Bill on
a rather windy day I
noticed lots of colourful
garden sheds square-cut
stone & smooth curvy
sea-washed stone frilled
with slippery weed I
stood on the Pulpit Rock

leaning into the wind & sea-
spray also couldn't help
noticing a block of dark grey
military conglomerate very
square edged indeed looking
as if the cliffs to its Westness
had actually lost something of

lumps I would
like to record
some of this
walk in some
poetry way I

themselves by ejection of

a writing window to get it down

a large part and that that
part had landed on the
ground above them and
then was perhaps carved
out by wee bipeds in
uniforms also noticed
lots of very large sugar

am continually
turning it over
in my mind
and hope to
get enough of

VEÄSTA

1. PORTLAND MIX

He's disturbed by laughing pensioners
as waves preach at the Pulpit -
a pale blue sky is patterned with cloud
and dark blue water meets the shingle line.
There's a view over paper-coloured stone
to Ladram Bay and Berry Head.

So he clambers ashore,
avoiding the Lobster Pot and the Hole In The Wall,
then slouches along the white cement track
past shanty huts with names like Bonny Mary -
in minutes, the claret band of the lighthouse
is aesthetic, like valerium or ragwort,
common scurvy grass, sea lavender or coltsfoot.

Lepidoptera lose their colour in the sky
from silver studded and chalk hill blue
to grayling, burnet moth and skipper.
The sky becomes a butterfly on the monster's nose
and bay trees can't prevent his witchcraft.

So they sling stones at the kimberlun
with a red beard and a coxcomb
whose half yard legs had stood in the shallows
as he bowed before vanishing,
five hundred years ago -
each year since a cloud of unknowing.

He continues to walk where I follow.
My following makes him walk
past the Eight Bells at Southwell,
abandoned smashed-up digger-crabs,
sheep like blocks of stone from Perryfield,
Perryfield blocks like sheep from cloud-lodes,
up Wakeham's wide white street -

like dove's wing or gander's wing,
that creamy, cloudy stone
whose halva-streak in the hand
spells I Love Shane as the bus bumps north
to the yellow-grey roofs of Chiswell.

The return of the Absent Lord
is marked by the sound of copters
whirring over the tidal mere,
where sheep were washed
and staffs incised by the reeve
guarded underhill and tophill.

He comes to release the inmates,
to baptise the island -
follows a urine tang
through brambles, blackthorn, privet.
But this place is carved from a single stone,
each aunt or uncle tight as a pebble,
like not speaking to like -
just getting on with the business.

On this muteness of an island
where a rabbit's the worst of luck,
there's a need for a rooster's voice
to supplant the twittering
of greenfinch and linnet,
skylark and wheatear,
chaffinch and pipit,
rustling of mice, badgers, foxes,
barley, corn and wheat.

But what does it mean to speak *for* -
when language rises out of landscape
from the lungs of an intruder?

Still, he comes at my behest
to be stoned from the island,
for secreting seed in the white one's womb
whilst choosing the chastity of the uninvolved
against the arrow-suited stupor of the married -

he dwindles as he exits
in a hail of hard white clods,
beneath the bulbous gaze
of the golf-balled heights.

2. INTERLUDE: SLINGS AND ARROWS

Across the limestone plateau,
the Potala of compulsion squats
where pig-eyed window-slits
conceal the crew-cut brethren

who can pile stones in water,
dumb in arrowed suits,
six million tons over twenty-three years
without a word in jest.

As stone number seven million
seven hundred and one is placed
in the mouth of the bay,
the monster surfaces,
mirroring muteness -
stones the size of fists
and fists the size of stones
are both compact
and meaningless.

There is too much time to say nothing.
A stone is a stone is a crumpled sheet,
exists at the bottom of the sky -

but the reddish gaze of Weymouth
silences the glance.
A hundred years later,
a Brummie family debates -
a camcorder purrs
in the hands of kimberluns
recording the shadows of work.

The boy sent back for another gallon
never returned - he crossed the bar,
exhausted by the stench
of urine from fields,
cold tea in flasks
at Independent and Trade,

was exchanged for a slave in an arrow suit
who is really a Tibetan monk,
chants Om Mani Padme Hum
as water's dammed,
as language ceases to flow.

3. GIBRALTAR MIX

Monkeys shriek
as the monster accompanies his demo tapes,
informing them that he is not mad,
that he is not a fool, that this *is* the place,
his eyes as hollow as the rock.

He clutches a visa in his hand,
an old bus ticket over-stamped with Spanish -
language adopted in response to the threat
from Algeçiras and Melcombe Regis.

Light catches the cranes of Gibrepair.
The cable-car rises past him to the top
where the view includes the far-off Atlas Mountains
and the airport to the right of Chesil Beach.

Painted black, he is a mountain shadow
despite his blonde hair's hayrick -
he has left his fame at the border
and wanders, twanging his guitar.
The water's a swimming pool blue.
He strides with an orange in his pocket
and a stash of tablets in his hand.

There are 24,000 offshore institutions,
one for every aunt and uncle.
Under the Tower of Homage,
the pubs stay open day and night
as invisible tails of monkeys
flick the monster's mug.

Caruna and Bossano
chase cigarette smugglers
through dead end quarry paths,
through brambles, blackthorn, privet -
pelted by hard white clods of limestone,
they ride the crest of the rockwave.

Parasite, he turns
the island to an audience -
the reaction of the apes
is destined for the archives.

He scrounges his way through the landscape,
pursued by agents and minders,
homing in on the Rif,
the Master Musicians of Jajouka
as if he could vault the straits.
Earth's shadows fly as birds head south -
under *a dome of many-coloured glass*
his vision comes and goes in colours.

In the overgrown Trafalgar cemetery,
an inscription celebrates Juan Malefico.
Monstrous songs express the island,
despite the apish cries of squaddies and sailors
and myriad shades of silence
hauled from the throats of inmates.

His fur coat's extra-terrestrial.
He roams in a plain white kaftan,
about to awaken *from the dream of life*
and *unrest which men miscall delight*
in a dove-cloud over a park.

The publicans and dockers
are getting on with their business.
The border fastens like a zip
past the helicopter pad.

He picks up a stone -
a plectrum made of moonish marble.
He wants to describe this island
with an album, not a single.

He wants. Wants love.
Wants another blonde-haired mirror.
To be spoilt and float,
this interpreter, this coxcomb lyrist.

Then soft sky smiles,
condenses him
to an instant star-soul
as the cranes catch light.

4. INTERLUDE: A SPOILT BOY PONDERS

He sits where butterflies have lost their blue,
where stones have turned to misericords,
where the dumping of old cars
is treated as a mainland insult,
where the name of the hole in the ground,
be it Bowers, Broadcroft, Kingsbarrow or Yeolands
is invisible to the eyes
of this spoilt boy pondering his failure,
who is nowhere near ready for success
as he knows deep down beneath his hayrick hair.

The century's hottest summer
blackens his brow.

Sun surrounds him,
sunny side up and down.
Rock's as warm as sky.
Great furnace doors have opened.

He would like to find the body he caresses,
not here, not now, but his many sleepless nights
play through him as he sits, frowning,
sixteen years old and silent as the island,
connected to his family by a spit of pebbles.

But he does not like the island
because it is too close,
too physical, too naked.

It reminds him of the body
that is silent and unready,
that is whispered from him
into the mirror,

so confides his depression
to his parents,
is snubbed as an ingrate
as they take the side of the island.

Twenty years later,
he returns to sit here.
The body lies beneath him
and behind him and beyond him -
only the whiteness holds.

5. MALTESE MIX

Silent cities can be seen
across the limestone plateau
through a landscape stippled
with dead songbirds,
blessed by Our Lady of Victories -
a Sleeping Lady today
beneath the desiccated eye of Horus.

Dead songbirds tell no tales -
greenfinch and linnet,
skylark and wheatear,
chaffinch and rock pipit

cleave to a louder voice,
a priestly oracle with quiz predictions.

My following makes him walk
as hard clods hammer him -
globigerina, coralline.

Through the crooked streets of the island,
rabbits run before the pot.
Trapped for the national dish
they have no voice, just breath to offer.
They are incapable of praising.

Language rises out of the landscape
from the lungs of an intruder,
through the island's terraced fields
where a pair of sturdy legs and a pleated skirt
are as mute as the haunches of a suckling sow.

The workers get on with the work.
Hours go by and only the observer
scrounges his way through the landscape.

Valetta lies beneath the Heights.
Light catches harbour cranes
as seen from the Tower of the Standard,
through Judas Holes in the face -

and he lodges like a stranded mariner,
not far from the Inquisitor's summer palace,
having given good service
through the bureaucratic day,
he stares at the ceiling of his chamber,
his red beard untended and his spirits fading,
letting his blood turn ruby, as revellers shout
and the dogs dance with the pigs.

There are two clocks. One is correct -
this is the one that marks his passage.
The second is false, to fool the Devil -
this is the one by which he reckons.

And the homeland is absent…
dear Devon streams an unconsoling myth
in this land of low stone walls
and flat-footed locals.

The birds remain felled and the rabbits, stewed.
He regains some strength and begins to walk
the cart-tracks and high white paths,
watching, but not working now,
speaking for others who pick stones
from buff-coloured lawnsheds -
such a mild imperialist, this idler,
this interpreter, this coxcomb lyricist.

He strides, with an orange in his pocket
and a stash of olives in his hand.
He is parasite, he turns the world
to scribbles in a battered notebook,
destined for the archives.

And even the hypogeum cannot hold him -
spirals, hexagons, red ochre traces,
swirling patterns and the echoes of riddles.
The Sleeping Lady's face is as white
as globigerina limestone,
as coralline limestone,
as oolitic limestone,

as this creamy cloudy halva of limestone
that is ghost-rock,
moon-rock,
papyrus of indelible silence.

He takes what he needs -
condenses time and work
to these traces on a page.
The inmates look up briefly,
get on with the business
of their clod-hard lives.

6. INTERLUDE: THE BODIES LEFT BEHIND

Each year was a cloud of unknowing
and Leland called the natives
strong, wilful, somewhat avaricious.
Rain swept in from the Channel.

Above the Lower Purbeck Beds
they rode, on the saddle of a monster
only partly exposed
out of winter rain and fog.

It almost ceased to exist
on dark November days
when a drool of soggy stones
connected it to the world.

Stone. Pearce. Comben. White.
A limited range of surnames -
nicknames distinguished
aunt from uncle.

They tested the seed
before they married,
lived healthy lives
before they pickled,

worked twelve-hour shifts
as silver studded and chalk hill blue,
grayling, burnet moth and skipper
cavorted briefly and vanished -

walked home in wind and rain
on winter evenings to their hearths
where rabbit stews swung richly,
their lives held steadfast and true.

There were story-tellers and balladeers -
affirmers of the visible,
articulators of the certain,
patrollers of limits,

and reeves with notched staffs
quantified the mist, kept kimberluns at bay
with their coxcombs
and their beards…

7. ADEN MIX

In this port of call
he paces like a prisoner -
distilled sea water
has turned to sweat,
in a place whose only resource
is salt.

The greens of Charleville are alien
to this place of doomsday fire
where Abel lies, an eternal creditor
in a squadron-whine of mosquitoes,
below Big Ben's dwarf replica
on the slopes above misfortune's well.

He has come to bury his past in gold,
to pay homage at the Tower of Silence.
He hates this horrible rock
but hears its call to prayer
above the muezzin
who marshals the inmates
against this interpreter,
this coxcomb lyricist.

He knows long residence
impairs the faculties,
and soon will dwell instead
amongst hyenas in Harar -
but he bides his time
as sunlight moistens
the harbour's eye,
its cargo of fins and maws.

As ever, *the black moons*
follow the white
on a creamy cloudy stone
as dry as cuttlefish ghosts,
as pure as mother of pearl, and yet
as bitter to the soul as aloes.

He strides with a scoop
of arabica in his pocket
and an invoice in his hand

but, despite
the businesslike tone of his voice,
he is still the *voyant* who responds
to the spray of approaching vessels,
in a time of assassins let loose.

Passing the hospital, he notes
his return in a decade's time,
leg bound and hoisted to the ceiling,
back flayed by immobility -
King Solomon about
to expel him from the high ground
to roast in Hell as if in a kiln.

He walks through that time and on,
distilled in spirit and eclipsed in flesh,
past Humbers, Rileys and Morris Minors,
sea creatures at the Lax Stores
lacquered like his reputation -
yet resists, as density's transgressor,
as traders keep on trading,
just clinging on to their businesses.

In Aziz's Bookshop,
he leafs through Z-Cars Annuals
to recover the notes he made and left
where beached shells strew the graves.

He is observing weightlessly -
as Cubans exit, Pizza Hut goes up
and speculators price
the view from Steamer Point.

But he returns, to pace
and sweat in his impatience,
cursing these days
with the glare of a dugong.

Birds lose voice
and fall into the Cisterns.
Best move on, he thinks
from a place where even the water rots
and whiteness is sepulchral.
He still thinks like a writer -
but his writing in this place
is in the nature of his silence

as language rises out of the landscape
and the lungs of intruders
rise and fall.

8. PORTLAND MIX (REPRISE)

But *every writer is a fraud*
and every traveller a scrounger
says a rabble-rouser in the Quarryman's Arms
to a crowd of armed quarrymen
as they cradle clods in their hands.

I wipe myself from the landscape
my following made him walk
and now he's on his own
as lanterns are lit
by the lynch mob.

The virtuous have copyrighted fury.
They mistrust the observer
who is surely idler, nonce or spy,
who distorts the silence they believe in,
who appropriates their names and actions
on the strength of a bus ride or a stroll -

who is self-obsessed when harmless,
drugged and crazed when dangerous,
who obliterates what he describes,
etherealises work and vaporises stone…

So they chase the Veästa back
down the road to the Bill and past the shanty huts
with names like Bonny Mary and beyond the Lobster Pot
like *a stag, a runnable stag*
past the claret band of the lighthouse -
his coxcomb flaps in the wind,
his half yard legs are wobbling
and his beard is matted as he runs.

And he jumps from the Pulpit,
tumbles from the island,
crashes against the water,
comes to rest and floats.

Beneath a dark blue sky
with indifferent stars, he bows
before vanishing once again
for five hundred years or a day.

Pontoon 6. *Escape practice... Skimming tones...*

Flatmate on prison ship clowns around with revisionists.
Massaged an oil tanker as Geronimo charged a tape-recorder.
My tongue was raw but at least the ploughing got done.

My Esperanto was raw but at least my hare had 3 earrings.
I thought of one thing once so I thought of another.   *Orbital hippy*
Thinking's quite unlike doing one thing then doing another.   *Shell sandwich*

Don't forget the pulsing silk Portuguese amnesiacs.
Sachets of DNA in jammy glitz garlanded with dusk at dawn.
Weed tassels hang from hair-of-the-dog. Blood-rush to mask.

A bundle of those bargains and a pack of those stickers please.
Sprigs to commemorate crash in the subway sprout early.   *Time slip blip*
Ribboned-off rock-fall. Councillor dressed as petrol pump.   *Backdrop drops*

The glossematic sea gives a thumbs-up to allies on tap.
We waz zinking in ze wind. Those zunk hermetically oozed.   *Inverted D-Day*
Jobs scuttle your face. Face blossoms from a force ten kiss.

Daily from school bus window I saw a wall of rounded stones
keeping the sea on the rough side from falling
into the sea on the calm side. It was a war
between castles and tanks. Sailors dressing up
as soldiers then blowing up their own ships.

a per
imiter of
a mil
itary list
ening stat
ion deco
rated with
a jag
gedy-top
ped fence

giant Christ
mas tin
sel pain
ted Port

land pale

From the top of the big wheel he could see over the Bastille.
From inside the microcosm he could desensitise a landslide.
Candidates spidery wives playing football on fairy ferry.

The assassin froze prior to basking in the pathology.
His Auntie Flo trapped in amber. Cucumber in cotton tatters.
Better off than a pipe's neck stuck out like an anvil horn.

This was a stolen book made with stone then truth drugged.
Humming could be heard – footballer wife wiv talking library bk.
Chorister lays down a trail of jewels. Spatted white cadet.

Landscape was something seen from coaches not busses.
 Taut trips... Retinal foundations... Lacanian charm...

Flan filled with mucous. Indeterminacy and a migrant eye.
Discourse with your eyes onto off-course crypto planets.
Fall behind H.M.S. Tenebris to ahoy the privateer Paris.

Becalmed in the truth the dominant monad trades sextants.
Marsh swan divides rush hour into two slang children.
Knowledge tossed overboard. Sleep in our dream.

The young are impressionable and bitter. System trash.
When I was young the ocean's mystery was ground down.   *Field Ground*
Grains taken to the all-night pharmacy to be grammared.   *flat as a*
                                                             sea urchin that's
The gulf between flotsam and jetsam cannot be fetishised.   *swallowed a*
Ice cream albatross and Nietzchean utility - not in the notes.   *gobstopper*
Apply pressure to my Dad and he'd admit breaking rocks.

Albion's Uncertainty Principle

below the cricket field
there's a cavern   full

of thick inpenetrable
black space   when

the work-lights
are   out   other

                       wise there

's an array
of un   der

ground   gall
eries all daz

zling white
em   pty

                  squa
                  red[2]

today the cricketers wear
their   oolitic   whites

the cricketers stand stock
still   in the sunshine   a

                                 bidingby
                                 the rules
                                 of   geo

            logi   cal
            time   the
            very thin

Portland Stone of
their shirts   &
trousers   being

       very very very
       gently ruffl ed
       by the off -sea

breeze makes
one combined

           distinct stone
           sound   a

gentle sesame-opening
sepulchre-stone grind
so same so   third-day

rising so oh
&   one   so
rolling   so

       different   A   perfectly

       round smooth white   a perfect

       brilliant pale   orb   a glorious

       ball of Torpandl Stone   hangs

(heaven knows) far out in deep space as a bit o' split willow tree like a stang or even a penis swings through silence's still un

                til BANG

Pontoon 7. *Slung umbrella… Minus 1000 plateaus…*

Memory is driven into a trap by what we might call a step-memory.
  The Bromige poem reduced this flooding of the heart
    to a simple yet adjustable trauma that could, in turn,
      change all debasing generics into
        a fossilised transformer toy.

Low flying dragon only just cleared the breakwater.
We played where there'd been a rape and there'd be another.
Sailors all vanished from the universe in one prodigious dither.

The exiled prayer materialised. Moby Dick at the school fete.
Waist high in vault the sniper fired across the school field.
The orphans held their picnic thoughtlessly on a differential abyss.

Reef litter. Tugboat regatta on lagoon of alcoholic brine.
Sanitary flags kink in east weir breeze. Invasion phony.   *Launched Avalon*
Lyotard's *Just Gaming* first prise in local rag competition.

Trophies in the window. Obscure victories. Sniffles.   *Space divers*
The consolation of trophies when windows come in second.
Phenomenological runners-up. Rectitude sprawl.

Beast made with fallen leaves and rotting sand jumps sideways.
gOD made with fallen beasts. Suits trembling on their hangers.
Weep into the well and shiver in the river of air.

Sketch of Pennsylvania Castle done with paint stripper.
A whale of a time ends up beached and butchered.   *Vacant hermitage*
In the grey fathoms of the open quarry we veil our thoughts.

an i comes a
cross all
vicarly braced a
gainst a sea-spray a
top A Pulpit Rock

pray un preach all

you will un your

        will will

be done un

sea will si(gh)

        lence

Take that smirk in two hands then college scarf twist it.
Was in two minds but the caves joined up - they wuz sea caves.
Walked miles to your funeral but swam in your wake.

The holy-water bottle stopper was longer than the bottle.   *Ship in*
The water was longer in the bottle than in the antic body.   *holy water*
Aloof priest unfolds a map of Dorset made of loofah fibres.   *bottle*

Painlessly butchered. The boxer punches his sweet doves.
Wrecks rudely spit and rue daylight. Barber clips my sails.
Muscular Olla Podrida geologically lax in a bathing cap.   *Baling out*

Liberals help themselves to a washed-up crate of oranges.   *Walking the bike*
Embodied in disguised war. Pressed salvage-crew.   *through froth*
Bastard godsons zapping TV in search of post-modernity.

Drove 200 miles to see the fairy-lights swing in the Square.   *So it's silly*
Long hair dwarfed by the giants in the health food shop.   *AND serious then -*
If I'd gone into academia could I decipher a prolapsed text?   *The Jurassic Cost*

It Is On A

Port
land

Isle an I now
walks on a

point pulling
ids is a

land's porpoise a

picking @
sea-threads

that's a point
a port of

call a
place all

eyes set
sales

for & from

my I your I
& I I

cap
stone

foamy lines form
ulating a

proof

rocks on
sea's wobble

ululating with one's
oolitic tongue

neath your eyes
patiently on

water's table

form ululated get
it/It

I am form
a form

(foam)

from for a
was not
to be will

an id
on a pin

on a pale
spindle o'

(g)round

a splinter
of white

bone pokes
Mary's vast

blue

wrinkling shif
ty robe o

my my
my other

not otter nor
mother

portland
stone blank

as paper a

poor poet po(u)res

over a

point of a no

re

turn

Pontoon 8. *Surplus engagement... Thrown keyhole...*

This is like one of those humorous history books for kids:
Vicious Vikings and Vile Victorians etc.
No fetish is entirely intelligible - practical yes.
Surrealism argued about the blueprint's Mod delicacy
when the island barged - legally, as in football -
into an international language.

Friction. Then clogging. Then sprawling and venting.
A mock town. Fog dematerialised instants into forgetting.   *The St. Stephen mix*
Portland was made of madness and erudition not rock.

The ghost ship reflection in the flecks of our eyes.
Mirrored stilts. Bilge. Mattery seats for humpy spiritualists.
Smacking of the indigo wind on a cramped impediment.

The smell of the island under the sea. Dealt a wild card.
Bright brown bomb crater on the bank behind our house.   *Rapid*
Even in the centre of the sun there are a few icy chills.   *understanding*

Going to be a cowboy while there are still cowboys left to be.
Romantically shoot a buffalo before they all get shot.   *Medicine spoon*
Chalk the mark of Zorro on the leaking graves of the poor.   *dissolves*

Corrugated angst iron. Sea-blue city swells a green belt.
Digital fish collide in rainbow dunked in kaleidoscope.   *Oars chop fish*
Well refracts a parallel hell. Time bomb in a coma.   *into meat*

Natives re-enact a bit of stage habit. Masonic skateboard.
No sacked suburb. In the trenches of sleep all are flogged.
Lady gives kidney to her one and only as a gesture.   *Just kidding*

No revolution. No authority. No strained foreshore.
Garden of Eden regulated and controlled by a giant computer.
Silver horses imprint head massage. Driftwood black.   *Requiem Mass*
    for Space Capsule

Carved fossils from salt and sherbet. Corridor recluse.
You say to yourself this will do. I heard you say it mate.
Warships' old grey flesh hangs like a flag in the doldrums.

Ritual erodes ritual site. Ghastly secure box corrodes thug.
A priapic monster condemned to walking the coastal path.   *Gothic retina*
Turn. Face the sea. Always late though there's nowhere to go.

Junk shop open weekdays. Antique shop open weekends.   *The island's*
The rain comes down like loose-change from a playsuit.   *coffer*
Paralysed sailors dance and sing to the health of the Other.

This is serious disrespect. Musical chairs shunt and punt.   *Is it possible*
Semi-conscious furniture store votes for bigwig incumbent.   *to be castrated*
The guard-dog on the pontoon has eaten another apprentice.   *by a shockwave?*

on a limestone lip
four fat spars
of salted wood shackled

together with
          brown ir

    on

waiting to pull
a whole

planet out
from its

ocean

Is word association an acting chain or a one-to-one
with no vanishing-point? I associated seascape not with the sea
but with paintings propped against walls on Weymouth queue.
Saturday afternoon family trips into town were a signal
that the weight of the world was not constant -
the eye could fall anywhere - not a choice
of enlightenment or texture
but a pick between gravity and clockwork.

Blind spot flexes. Local author feeds off a bathing beauty.
The flat of the land. The rivulet. Long faced axiom.   *Forged passport*
Nothing grows here but decanters. Freudian ocean decay.   *Rotary Pope*

Hermes is a manure. Marx smiles inside a vacuum flask.
Stoned vampire snarls at garlic crusher in catalogue.   *Duchamp's boots*
Don't read too much into the ocean. It's not unbounded.   *Nobel Prize to*
                                                                                          Frankenstein

Darwin pours out Malcolm McLaren from the same flask.
Wolf evolves into furry red seat in dark Sunday night cinema.
Bingo caller got boarded-up. Horror. Channels of clobber.

Ooids

ground drew o
aeons before ids or
egos
who drew ids is
what not white
powdery robes
pale doors hoods or
hokeey oak put
a right light in
and take
double-oxygen-bon
ded-carbon out
sea (salty) shakes
it all a boat
of stone
at a spit's toe
at an isthmus-tip
at a vast stone
bird's beak's finish
sea-sheen on
pale pale
stone gleams
as smeared
mistletoe in moon
light
spit on
a twig
as a
thrush rushes
notes up
spit-globs lit
like pearls
hush thrush
pushes out
a kind o'
sonic calcitic goo
a mistle launch
five ... four ... three ...
(ear we go ear
we go ear (wig))
eggy fluids
pale white

stringy strands
pale white
standing stones
a ring o'
ids drew
eggs to
egos
shell shards rolled
round in lime mud
o a light so
brine-bright
nine dazzling
stones like
white fish
fingers stood
round stands
round will
stand round
(blasted out)
as sun fries egos
Albumen Stone
(not as sea meant)
all by on
some by
off come
by are
(blocks with drill
-serrated arêtes)
o 'ave a long
deep gaze down
in In
most
hay car
vers cleave
as wea
ther leaves
lithic (ithaca)
(t)ricks draw
/drew ids ill
usion (sion
(sigh on)
ion (icon)
& us) & deep
seep well

Pontoon 9. *David... Chris... Hans Heathen Anderson...*

Crossed the street to avoid the regional news. Blunt snare.
Vietnam and Torrey Canyon bribed back into the Cubs.
Drug cabinet abandoned in efflorescent quarry.   *Crawling bats*

Popular stencil

The waves travel outward from the shore. Alien lovers.   *Canned laughter*
Low tide reveals chariots exposed like shadows under boulders.
Unprofitable oneiric production line turned round by magnet.

During weekdays I left Portland to go to school in Weymouth.
  I was a Catholic. I lived two lives. This fostered
    aesthetic greed.

Drunk marine squares up to the oval void. Fists crawl.
Limbo spindrift deposit. Family Favourites clone.   *Creaking pontoon*
The times they are a changin' or transubstantiation w'out mirrors.

Logic spouts the lighthouse should have a rubbish bin.   *Totem pole was*
TV aerials were metal giants of geometry climbing into wind.   *sectioned*
Every house top-heavy. Shakespearian temptress frieze.

Rude philosophy of unidentified body in burnt maze.   *Crude futures*
War between the Co-op and Lipton's. Strawman skittle.
Champion the Wonder Horse fording the Lime River.

Proteins leak from *the mind like a sewer*. Lapsed universals.
Information in motto form ferries us to the chain-gang stars.
Film extras acting naturally until you notice their feet.   *Or their*

overflowing

Indulgence dump. Sputnik lands in Granddad's cabbages.   *lies*
Is hell-on-earth really disguised behind those prison walls?
Spitfire tunnels under H.M.S. Hood flying over unmolested.

Dad ran away to sea [as they say] by telling lies to authorities
  though he knew they could walk on water. He believed in
    their truth - a lesson learned in a dissociated state.
      It has something to do with why so many poems
        submitted to my magazine
          remind me of TV adverts.

a white red-striped light
house and at a very

most south

erly tip of

A B   ill a

chiseled oolitic obelisk

strong saline-screams

of wind cannot
move a notion

of my hair nor scrape
a no   cean

of my face nor

of yours as

a lite house b
ends and an

                        o

belisk dis

inter

g   rates to str

ands

of (c)

loud

Crucified antennae. The 50's home on the little 60's screen.
Penknives and adders. Spine-tingle charm of Cream's Badge.
Loplop thorned and roasted. Cold War spy in photo album.   *Sneaked out*
                                                                Sneaked in
Matchbox cars on riding mat stopped to fill-up with lighter-fuel.
Cut-away cargo. Genuine Pollacks turped off baseball boots.
Gretna Green dream. Doll's house garage. Balsawood fort.

Rotating pillows. Asthmatic spare-room woodworm spring.
On holiday inside a toy so huge you couldn't play with it.
Southampton was in Bristol. Portsmouth was in Plymouth.

Schoolboys throwing pebbles at drowning angels.   *Rebellious sleep*
Good at art? Back seat forbidden fruit? Metal defector.
Quantum mechanic gave my imagination an MOT certificate.

Weird hospital where nothing happens and nobody is ill.
The Atlantic an aerial photograph of English Channel evasion.
Eye-patches litter the road like a plain of slaughtered buffalo.

Tramp lives in council house made of empty dog-food cans.
Tramp dies in mortgaged cave. The horizon tilts.
Down the well a demon in a German helmet rapes the water.

The romance of going to sea is dependent on the romance
of coming home. A desire to join the Navy is not subliminal –
Venus, on the contrary, tends to aesthetically stain
her water-mark on the brain. War with Germany
was an advert without actors yet a company's reliance
on advertising is crucial to the theatre's survival.
Final Act opens with stage hands still placing pebbles.

Square-Round-Triangle   a Portland Bill   a May 2013

Tis easier for a poet to pass / thru thine eye's needle // than t'enter 'eaven! – Timothy Rope

a prolo   gue

a kimber
lun a ba

lancing lub
ber spies

from a
thin brit   (th)read

tle Durdle D
oor ridge

of cra
zed pale grey

oo

lite *Harb*
ourcount

ry Rock   thread

a rag
ged fuz

zy edged elon
gated sca

lene tria

ngle
a splin

ter a spit
a bone

sherd a bill

a wed | ge an | edge to | west | rests fast | on ho | rizon's | Bill a nee | dle and | Dur | dle door | an Eye | some deli | catly wobb | ling kim lubber | berlun must

Pontoon 10. *Resemblance... Rationalisation... Raw evasion...*

Spread Suzie Creamcheese on Lautreamont's flushed shark.   *Pier pressure*
Autistic tarbaby gone AWOL off the end of the candlelight.   *Wrong proof*
No man is an isthmus. The bell tolls for Lee (Harwood etc.)

Ripe Veasta chasing its own shadow into the casino.   *Respond time siren*
Anaemic salamander shops for chops at out-of-date hop.
Venus evaporates from bricked-up arch to marry sea-cadet.

Restless components. Rhythm-method. Tithonian rent.
Mondrian's pier swishes the surface plaster into ridges.   *Busy surfer*
Brewers of communion wine up-periscope into party dress.   *Celtic spirit*

The wonderer returns. Buys a black beer to pour over priest.
Ships passing in the night - identical micrite pensions.
Beachcomber finds hair-spray canister beside green-haired rock.

Lobster pots fill with pink sheet music. Pneumatic beauty.
The cult of personality ghostwrites a new sea shanty.   *Prefab Land Shanty*
Pubs communicate telepathically with calcite pincers.

Portland castle built in poxy Henry 8's pocket by proxy.   *Walk to work*
The space between travel and tourism is only eyelid deep.   *to get it*
Unplanned power. Inventory of sober impulses.

White Comben Stone Pearce Pearce Stone Comben White.   *Two teenagers*
Allen Dewland Cox. Names no more than words in drag.   *having a*
Indifferent storms' irregular norms. Autographed cement.   *discussion*

Den meant different to camp. Corrugated castle bomb crater.
Sliding in boxes down the dead yellow grass. Burning caress.
Brown from the sun and black from berries. Limping float.

Punish me master if you can point me out. Wreckers' lamp.   *Twist*
The past is a sceptical cure for a form of fashion schizophrenia.
Norman places and I play would be true if truth were a place.

Portland was never a place it was a parcel flying through ether.
Either ether or acid. And I never played there I coalesced.   *Bust*
We played other places. Teams hooked. Seahorse sappers.

Nearly 50 and still pondering what is called 'cause and effect'.
The abstraction called atheism was taught me by the stones,
the sea and a priest from Connemara in a bucking Triumph Herald.
I inherited a giant builder's yard full of concrete contradictions.
The heavy presence of stone was a hallucinogen of pure light yet
I'm a whetted appetite at most. Grace is material and the only thing
not made of it is language.

*

On To

Substitutes' ragshowlanguage/muffprecisionrelish//
skeletonshadowbe/hitchedsequenceon/spondulicks' get-
up-and-gostrawparlour//Sobladderoccupantsdream
tyres/incorrigiblet-shirtundividedlieu//explodetadpoles/
curlworldrafters/laterlineghost*urconscious*//ninter
flapped*either being*radio//theatrecrossroads' audience
simper/conquerors' bones//sleeveoncedust/peninsula
tabs' marlproxabeyancegloss//predicatedpoppedback
Featherwalk*blag*//*thingsswornchurch*faried

*language*Emergence//walkworlds/Boots
urpriseflush//seabeginstime *anothersays*
brand 'teaspratsbuggerproperty//real
everyone/arbitrationpetroglypheddoom
//anothertrousers 'blockrattingauger//
ourselvesforchangeBeach

*drawn elastic gun installation
instillation Semblance*

*Avalanche hat Gulp!
Daguerreotype of Intuition*

subs B Elizabethan cork

*misleading experience Knowledge
Magazine foetus Coalhouse*

visible crusteyes/splinters 'slope//saddlebag
shape//edgeillegiblevacuum//friends 'haze
iris nearby/eveningStetdraper-voiced/separates
skirt-foaltorchlight//currentlongleghoots//
crabshatecleftsilence//stuffpanic//owlbootsexist

Fantomas cigarettes Instamatic

star the Humb the Hand
Lady Sea
grooms

engagementkidsetc. yeshelicac footballanguage/venting forgetting rock//eyesspiritual
ists' impediment/card-belts' chills//beshopoor/greenkaleidoscopecoma/island-floggedgest
ure/foreshorecomputerpack/ reclusematedoldrums' thug//path go/weekend'splay suitother punt-
councillorapprentice/one-to-one sea-queue-signal constant//choice-textureclockwork beauty- raffoo 's,
axiomdecay//flask-catalogueunbounded/flask cinema-clobber//snareCubsquarry//lovers flame-
magnet//Weymouthfosteredgreed-crawl-clone/mirrorsbinwind-frieze-maze/skittleriver-uni
versals//stars' feetcabbages' walls//unmolestedauthoritiesinstatessubmittedadverts screen
Badgefaded//lighter-fuelbootsfort/spring it//Plymouthangel'sdefectorcertificate//ill-evasion
buffalocans//'tilt'swaterromance/subliminalstain//Germanyrarelyreliance//survival agonsingi

really eyes search witch of Methodists 'Mirror /cat marries Stopes //
hippy sandwich slipping blip Dday / Ground a that's a gobstopper
//Avalon diver's hermitage in water-bottle / Indigestible froth bike
//silly then war Dissemination cave precinct //grass-wind glasses surface analogues infinity beach stationespres

Twist Bust

pressure-proof
siren surfer-spirit
shanty work it

AUTHOR'S NOTE TO *PONTOON*

I lived on the Isle of Portland until I was 20. I knew the cliffs, quarries, shores and secret niches of the place intimately. Growing up in an environment with such a unique character had something to do with my becoming a poet.

Pontoon was written in the early 90's with minor editing since. Its idiosyncrasy is part-and-parcel of issues of language and memory that I was starting to engage with and I am as happy now with the raw texture that experiment produced as I was then. In other long poems begun in the same period those issues went further but in *Pontoon*, because it is both *about* a *place* and a blatant evasion of being *about place*, the issues were acute. The floating sidesteps were my way of returning to Portland something of the strange experience of growing up there.

Pontoon and *Veästa* were written independently but putting them in one volume seemed a good idea. Norman and myself have long been friends but our work reflects quite different takes on place and meaning, one reason why putting the pieces together would be interesting. I found Norman's idea of the simultaneous likeness and unlikeness of different places a kind of complimentary outsider's echo of my internalised displacement. I was a native Portlander writing what Norman referred to as an 'askew psychological take on growing up on an island' while he approached the subject as an outsider with a focused topology.

We always wanted a third element, partly provided by Susan Duxbury-Hibbert's drawings, then in 2010 'radical landscape' poet Mark Goodwin said he would be delighted to contribute. Mark knew Portland but for this project made special trips, writing in situ. The resulting pieces fitted perfectly and we had our balance. The decision to arrange the elements as we have, with *Veästa* bracketed between the first and second halves of *Pontoon* through which Mark's pieces weave in and around, was made because both Mark and myself felt that the fragmentary nature of *Pontoon* invited this intrusion of blocks quarried from the place itself.

Tim Allen, July 2015

AUTHOR'S NOTE TO *VEÄSTA*

This sequence was written in Bristol in the late spring of 1998 and, in an earlier version, was published online in the no-longer available webzine *Wandering Dog* (http://freespace.virginnet.co.uk/wandering. dog/poetry.htm). It has been subject to light-touch revision in January 2015, almost seventeen years after the two visits to Portland that inspired it and at a distant remove from much of the source material. I've not been on Portland since, although this has nothing to do with the sequence and it's an omission I'm keen to rectify soon.

The 'Veästa' of Portland legend is a mythical monster, like a red-bearded cockerel with half-yard legs, which has allegedly appeared off Portland Bill in the distant past. Tim has suggested, plausibly in my view, that it might have been an oarfish - as he puts it in recent e-mail correspondence, "the oarfish, when it pokes its plumed head out of the water could be mistaken for a giant swimming chicken" (correspondence with the author, 20th January 2015). Whatever (or whoever!) occasioned its appearance off medieval Portland, it is the ultimate 'kimberlun' - the local word for outsiders, presumably derived from the word 'chamberlain' - and, in this sequence, is pitched against the 'aunts' and 'uncles' who are the autochthons of the territory. It also takes the form of the author, and of three historical personalities who appear in the Gibraltar, Malta and Aden mixes respectively.

Information has been taken from direct observation as well as a number of textual sources. Principally, these are the Rough Guides to England and Spain (Penguin): the AA Essential Guide to Malta and Gozo: Enid Starkie's biography of Rimbaud: and Tim Mackintosh-Smith's *Yemen - Travels in Dictionary Land* (John Murray, 1997). Italicised direct quotations are from Shelley (Section 3), Machen (4), Coleridge (5), Leland (6), Rimbaud - in translation (7) and Davidson (8).

In an earlier note, I explained that 'the sequence refers to analogous landscapes in order to compare them to Portland, so that it emerges, hopefully, as a distinct yet representative terrain. A post-structuralist approach to place is attempted, in which each place is presented as a phoneme in a global language of locations; defined, accordingly, by its affinities and differences rather than by its 'uniqueness'.'

Since I compiled that (somewhat earnest) note, the association of the sequence with Tim and Mark's poetry and with the illustrations by Susan A. Duxbury-Hibbert have set these analogous landscapes into another context... as has the explosion of information online, which would enable me to conduct a virtual visit to Portland with a few keystrokes and clicks of the mouse. Despite this, I'm happy to preserve this sequence as it is - not just in its own right, but as a precursor to much of the material included in my three collections *The Book of Bells and Candles* (Waterloo Press, 2009), *Aphinar* (Waterloo Press, 2012) and, in particular, *Dreams of the Caucasus* (Shearsman Books, 2010).

Norman Jope
Plymouth, January 2015

AUTHOR'S NOTE TO *WALKED ROUND THE BILL*

I have actually visited Portland twice ... although reading Norman's & Tim's Portland poems also very much felt like visiting. My first 'bodily' visit was decades ago, when I took my basic climbing instructor qualification on the limestone cliffs of Portland Bill. My second visit was in May 2013, after being invited by Tim & Norman to contribute (if not to the actual place) to the poem-places that are *Pontoon* & *Veästa*. Tim has mentioned how 'the fragmentary nature of *Pontoon* invited this intrusion of blocks quarried from the place itself.' The intrusive blocks referred to are my own workings, and so the invitation given to me to visit turns out to have become also permission to intrude ... perhaps to dig, and to chisel. Portland Bill is a very odd place: it is an amalgam of contradictions. It disconcerts. And because of the obvious military & prison presences there, I at times had a feeling of my being some kind of poetic enemy commando prowling ... or escapee crawling along the surface of a forbidden splinter poking out from some version of a Kingdom called England. Portland Bill is foreign yet not. One finds oneself intruding in a strange Homeland ... novel, yet deeply familiar somehow, and so even more strange for it. It makes questions swirl like surf. Is Portland perhaps a distorted fractal of Great Britain? Is the Bill a debt to the very geology of Nationhood? Am I really seeing and feeling things as they are on Portland ... or is Portland a Shire & a Mordor dreamt into one elsewhere? To begin with, the only grip I could get on the place was by placing my hands on the ancient stone. I'm very much a physical poet: a treader & toucher ... and I often bring back, or make illusions of bringing back, substance & weathers from places. Portland limestone is an irresistible solidity for someone who is a climber, and is also obviously a necessary material for builders. So, my (or hopefully 'our') poetic building blocks intrude with imagined actual substance, hauled with and through imagination from some actual place. I am also a poet that often can't resist the substance of text – the texture, the stuff of speaking-&-writing – and so inevitably I quarried into both Tim's & Norman's poems. I gleaned and re-mixed gravels & sediments, then compressed the gleanings into blocks of alter-ego poems ... touchable stone(s) left in imaginations' flows to be, I hope, re-eroded by readers ... and re-built again by them ...

Mark Goodwin, Leicestershire, August 2015